THE BEST OF
KEVIN OLSON

BOOK 1

D1603922

Contents

A Dinosaur in My Backyard

Music by Kevin R. Olson
Lyrics by Julia Olson

from *Simply Silly!* (FF1300)

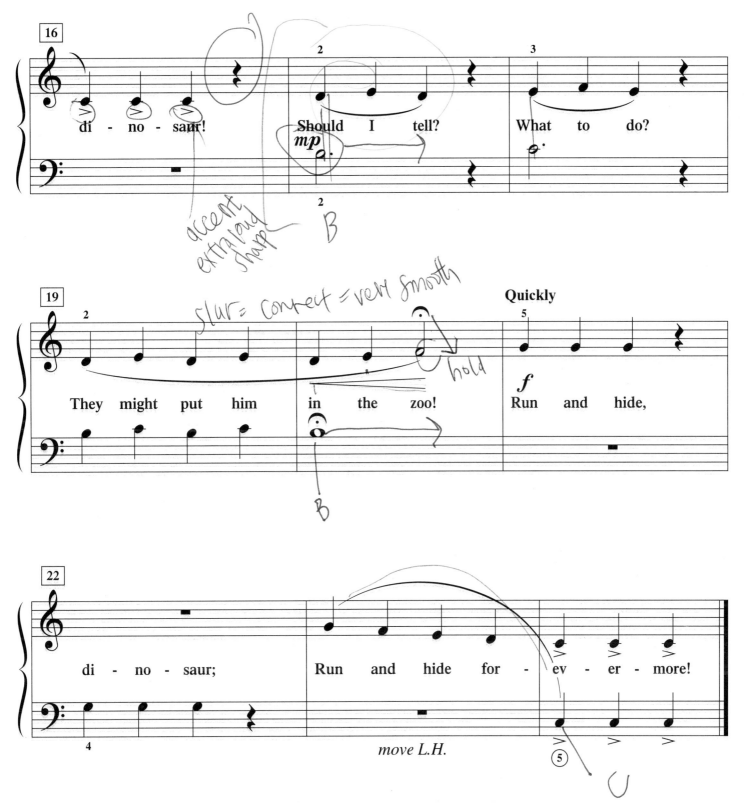

Scary Larry

a *written for you* piano solo (W9109)

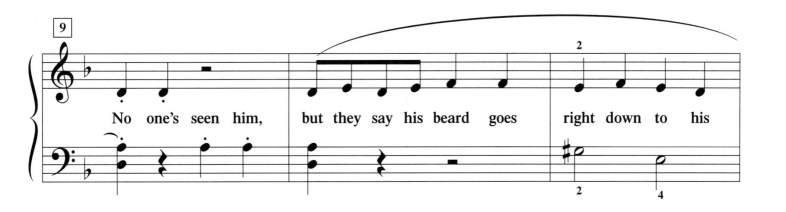

No one's seen him, but they say his beard goes right down to his

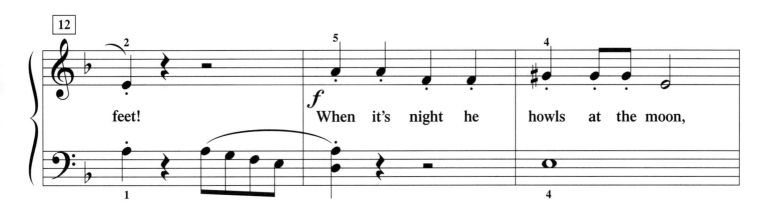

feet! When it's night he howls at the moon,

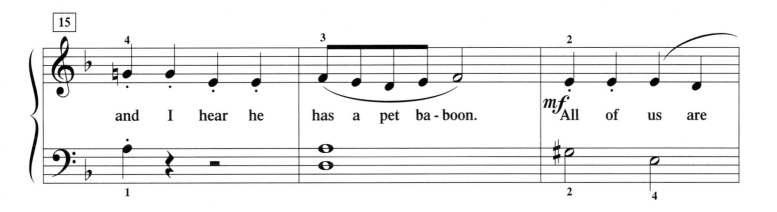

and I hear he has a pet ba-boon. All of us are

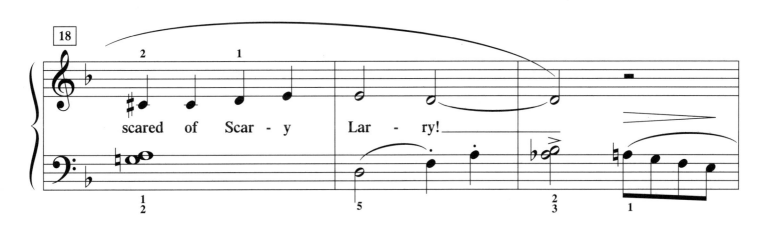

scared of Scar - y Lar - ry!

21

mp

p

Lar - ry just might

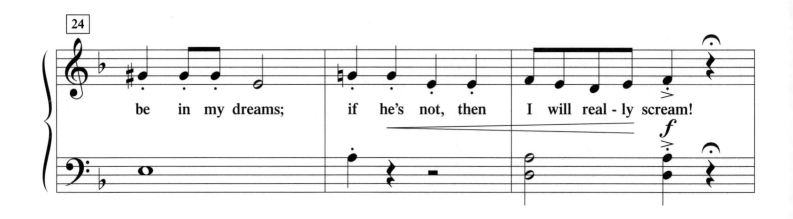

24

be in my dreams; if he's not, then I will real - ly scream!

f

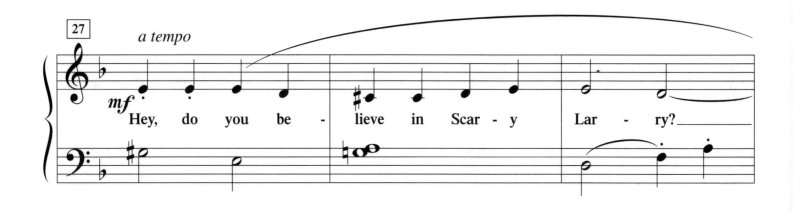

27

a tempo

mf

Hey, do you be - lieve in Scar - y Lar - ry?_____

30

3
2

p

f

3

Rolling Peas

from *Simply Silly!* (FF1300)

The Hermit Crab Cha-Cha

a *written for you* piano solo (W9013)

9

FF1324

10

FF1324

11

Somethin' Spicy

Fast and peppery! ($\quarternote$ = 208 or faster)

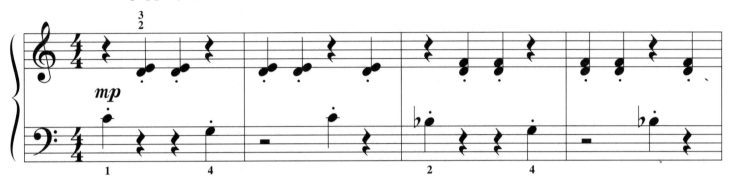

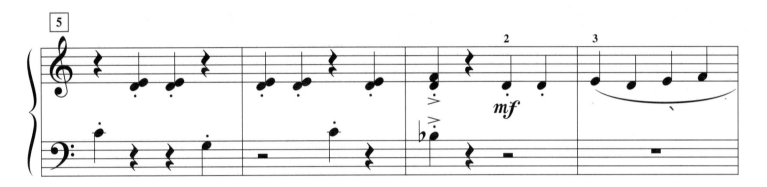

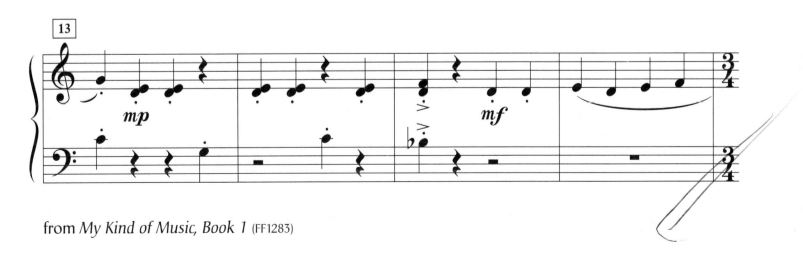

from *My Kind of Music, Book 1* (FF1283)

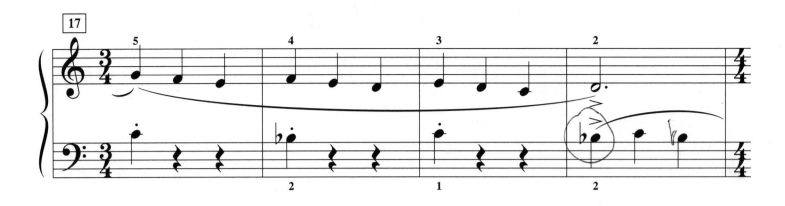

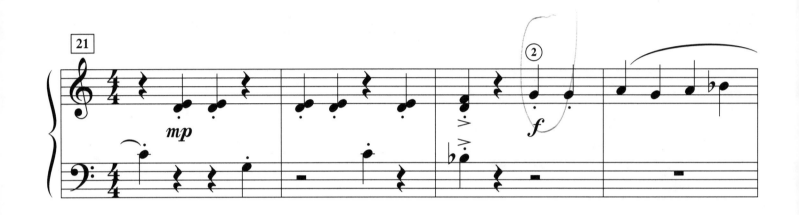

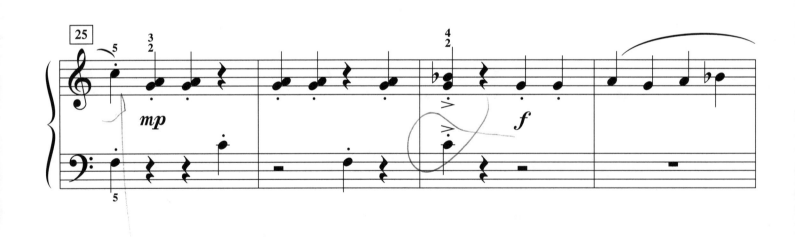

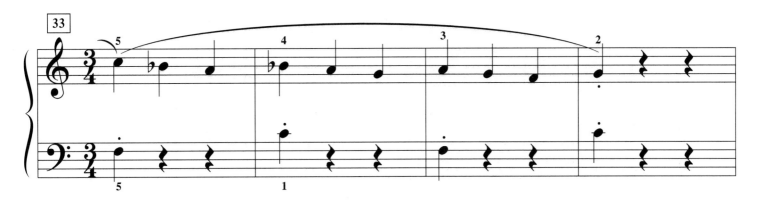

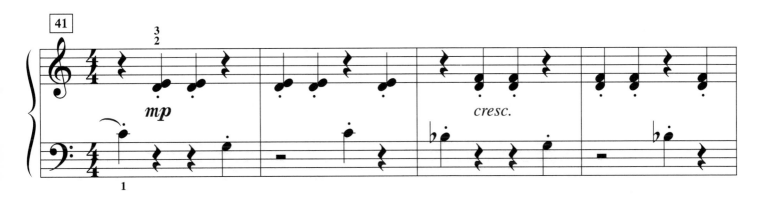

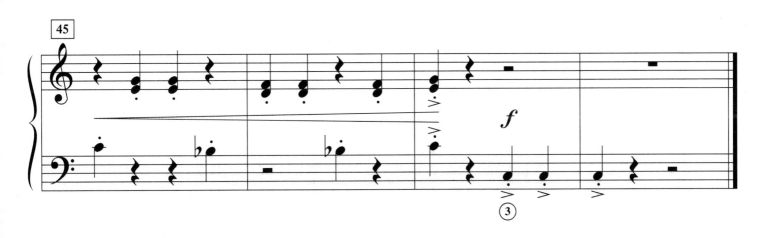

13

FF1324

14

Island Song

from *My Kind of Music, Book 1* (FF1283)

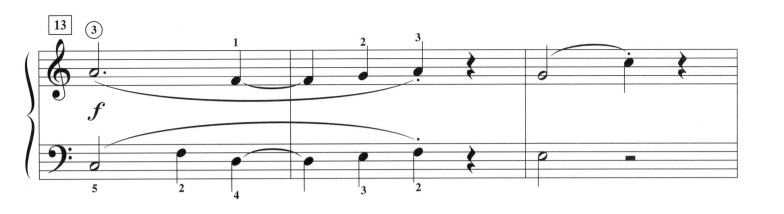

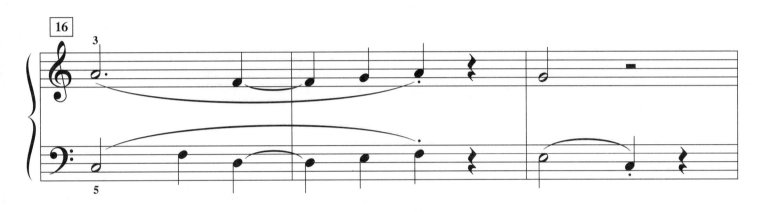

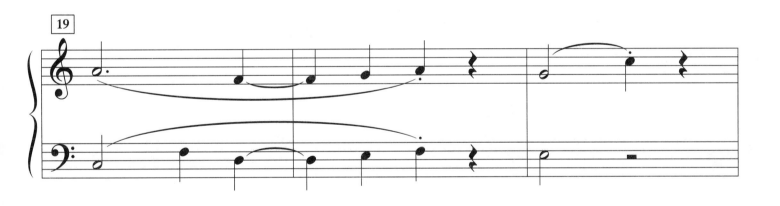

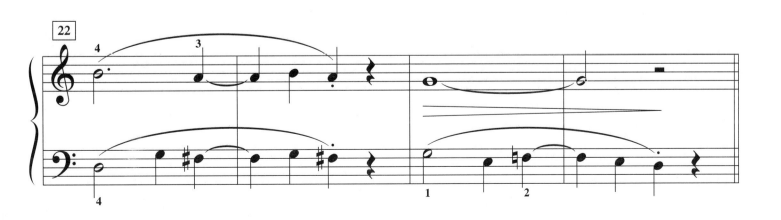

16

The Secret Agent

What job could be better than a secret agent? You get to ride in fast cars,
visit exotic places, and meet interesting people. Keep the piece full of energy and
excitement by keeping your staccatos sharp and your tempo steady.

With energy (♩ = ca. 192)

from *Showcase Solos, Book 1* (FF1125)

FF1324

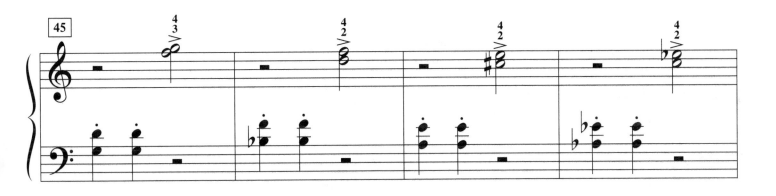

Nocturne

*A nocturne is a type of music that brings images of a peaceful night. There is usually
a tranquil melody over a constant accompaniment. Bring out this melody in the R.H.
It's kind of hidden, so follow the* tenuto *("stress") markings as you perform this "night music."*

from *Showcase Solos, Book 1* (FF1125)

Elephant Stomp

a *written for you* piano solo (W9042)